BABYNAMES

Picking the perfect name for your new arrival

Contents

Text by Claire Fletcher & Lisa Simpson.
Originally published in 2009 by L&K Designs. This edition published for Myriad Books Limited in 2010.
© L&K Designs 2009
PRINTED IN CHINA

Publishers Disclaimer

Whilst every effort has been made to ensure that the information contained is correct, the publisher cannot be held responsible for any errors and or omissions.

WHAT'S IN A NAME? THAT WHICH WE CALL A ROSE BY ANY OTHER NAME WOULD SMELL AS SWEET;

William Shakespeare (1564 - 1616)

Whilst Shakespeare may have implied that names are not that important, they send out a message to the world about our individuality, and last a lifetime, so bestowing a positive name is one of the most important gifts you can give your child.

The responsibility of baby-naming can overwhelm expectant parents. In times gone by, parents were more limited in their choice of names, and religious and traditional family names were the norm. Modern parents feel more obliged to choose a name that expresses individuality and this coupled with the greater diversity of names from which to choose can bring its own peculiar brand of pressure. This book will equip you with the tools to pick the perfect name for your offspring, and gives you a fun taster of the wealth of names out there.

It's vital to start researching baby names early and, if you are in a relationship, it is important to involve your partner in compiling a shortlist. You may be surprised at how much your attitudes to baby names differ: You might love flamboyant names and be dismayed to discover that your partner favours short names. It would be wise to talk through any differences of opinion before delivery day.

Don't fall into the trap of divulging your "contenders" to inquisitive friends and relations. A positive reaction to a potential name may make you feel unduly bound to it.

Remember when baby comes along it may look like another name altogether! Keep any controversial choices under your hat until baby-naming day. Few people would openly criticize your decision then!

Don't feel obliged to announce baby's name as soon as he or she arrives. The first few days after childbirth are hormonal and you might need a few days becoming familiar and comfortable with your choice before going public.

TOOLS TO HELP YOU CHOOSE THAT PERFECT NAME

There's a lot of valid advice on how to select a name. Consider the recommendations, but ultimately if you feel strongly that a name is right for your baby then follow your heart. You need to ask yourself: "What is most important to me and my baby in a name?" If you can answer that question then you are already halfway towards pinpointing the perfect name. Perhaps you will recognize in the following scenarios, your own personal set of expectations from a name...

I want to give a unique name that will help my child stand out from the crowd

If you are set on a rare name then do your research – trawl the many name dictionaries and see what overlooked pearls you can find. Study historical figures, mythology, the arts and other areas of knowledge for inspiration. Think about places or elements of nature that have aroused strong feelings of awe or admiration in you. If you are really brave you could create a name – perhaps using parts of names you love, hyphenating names or taking an attractive maiden name. There is a lot to be said for an unusual name but do remember that there is a difference between a special name and a name so wacky that it exposes a child to ridicule.

Remember that this is about your child not about showing the world how clever you are!

I want my child's name to sound beautiful and musical

Some people adore sharp snappy names like Zak, whilst others prefer the "music" of the longer Zachary. There's a lot to be said for a beautiful sounding name, though bear in mind that occasionally the name's meaning may not match up:

Malory trips off the tongue but actually means "unfortunate". Think carefully before giving your child a "pet" name solely because you like the sound of it. Whilst cute as a child it might lack gravitas in later life.

I want my child's name to reflect our cultural origins

There are many international name dictionaries in which to research an appropriate name to celebrate your baby's cultural heritage. You may want to honour your baby's forebears by bestowing a traditional family name or appropriating a maiden name as a first name.

I am looking for a spiritual name or a name with a positive meaning or message

Names can express some wonderful qualities and virtues, such as strength or beauty or hope; they can express spirituality or a term of endearment. If you are looking for a specific meaning then you will almost certainly find something fitting if you do your research.

I am searching for a name to signify something very personal and unique about our baby

Choosing a name that conveys the circumstances of your baby's conception, birth or appearance is a lovely way to tell their "story". Imagine your baby is delivered amidst a raging storm so you call her Thora after the Norse thunder god! Or your baby boy is born with glorious red hair so you name him Rufus ("red-haired" in Latin).

Some people may name their baby after the place that their baby was conceived or born. Other circumstances surrounding the birth can be acknowledged, such as the birth month (May), the day of the week that baby was born (Dominic), and their birth order within the family (Primo).

I want my child's name to honour an inspirational person or special place in my life

You may want to name your child after somebody you admire, love or respect – perhaps a cherished grandparent. You may wish to celebrate the power and beauty of our planet in your own little "force of nature" (consider Dawn, Oceana, Summer). Perhaps you wish to name your child after a place that arouses powerful emotions or which has a spirit that you wish your child to emulate (for example, Savannah, Skye, Nevada). If the names of those things that are dear to you are not so pleasing on the ear (sporting heroes and teams spring to mind here) then consign it to a middle name.

Once you have chosen your contenders, the following checklist will help you whittle down the list:

Consider the full name, and its permutations

Read the full name aloud to check that it sounds "right". See whether the initials look good on paper. Some combinations just look and sound better than others. This exercise will also rule out the remote possibility of unintentional comic effect.

We've all heard stories of people saddled with joke names such as Justin Case and Jo King, which seem scarcely credible. These extreme cases illustrate the importance of checking the name from all angles, including potential future nicknames.

So Patrick Nutter sounds fine but P. Nutter on an official form would be embarrassing. Likewise maybe Jo King started off life as the unremarkable Josephine King until someone decided to call her Jo.

Popular names

Do check your area's statistics for popular names, and give serious thought to eliminating choices which are in the top ten. Think ahead to how your child might feel about sharing a common name with classmates. If both your choices are ubiquitous, you could create a hyphenated or hybrid name. So for Lily and Anna you might substitute Liliana.

If your heart is still set on a particular name then consider other options. Your reasons for liking the name will hold the key to the solution. So someone who loved Jessica purely because they wanted to call their daughter the pet name Jess and weren't bothered about the name's meaning, may also like Jessamy (meaning "jasmine").

Parents who wanted to name their daughter Rose because of its literal meaning, but weren't so adamant about the sound of the name, might be happy to substitute one of the many international variations: the Italian Rosa or the Irish Roisin to name just two. If you love both the sound of the name and the meaning, then you might consider a subtly alternative spelling – so think Elinor for Eleanor. Reserve a little caution before going mad on alternative spellings though, as you may be setting your child up for a lifetime of explanations and misspellings!

At the end of the day, you may love the name so much that nothing will induce you to alter it. Nothing else feels right. If so, then go for it!Hopefully the above pointers will help you approach the baby naming quest with confidence. Here follows an eclectic list of names – a digestible taster of the thousands of names out there. Perhaps one name will spark off a particular avenue of research.

Choosing a baby name is fun if approached the right way. Think of the wealth of dictionaries and lists as a treasure chest. Hidden amongst them is a gem – the perfect name for your baby!

Abigail (F)
A biblical, Hebrew name meaning "joyful".

Abraham (M)
This name means "father of many", and is of Hebrew origin.

Adam (M)
A Hebrew name meaning "man". According to the Bible, Adam was the first human, created by God from the earth.

Angel
A name of Greek origin meaning "messenger of God".

Antonio (M)
A Spanish and Italian form of Anthony. The meaning of Antonio is unclear, however it is associated with goodness, being the name of a third century saint who founded Christian monasticism.

Antony (M)
Derived from the ancient Roman family name of Antonius (a famous member of which was the general Mark Antony).

Benjamin (M)
From the Old Testament, Benjamin is a Hebrew name meaning "son of the right hand" or "son of the south", or "son of my old age".

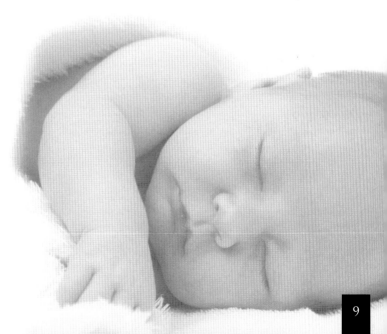

Caleb (M)

This Hebrew name means "dog" and represents faithfulness and courage. In the Bible, Caleb is one of only two Israelites, from amongst the many who leave Egypt with Moses, who succeeds in finally reaching the promised land.

Callum (M)

This is a Gaelic form of the Latin name Columba, meaning "dove", the symbol of peace and gentleness. Saint Columba was a sixth-century Irish missionary who was behind Scotland's conversion to Christianity.

Christopher (M)

Meaning "the bearer of Christ", this name is Greek in origin. Saint Christopher is the patron saint of travellers.

Daniel (M)

Of Hebrew origin, meaning "God is my judge". In the old Testament, Daniel was a Hebrew prophet living in Babylon where he served in the court of the king, interpreting his dreams. He was persecuted for his faith in God,which kept him alive in a den of lions.

Danielle (F)

Of Hebrew and French origin, and its meaning is "God is my Judge". Feminine variant of Daniel.

David (M)

Of Hebrew origin, meaning "beloved". In the bible, David was a shepherd and write of Psalms. St David is the patron saint of Wales.

Deborah (F)

A Hebrew name meaning "bee". In the bible Deborah was a prophetess who summoned Barak to battle against an invading army.

Delilah (F)

Of Hebrew origin, meaning "languishing, lovelorn, seductive". In the bible, Delilah was the woman who beguiled Samson into revealing the secret of his superhuman strength.

Dominic (M)

Of Latin derivation, Dominic means "of the lord" and traditionally it was bestowed on children born on a Sunday.

Elijah (M)

A Hebrew name which means "Yahweh is God".

Elizabeth (F)

Elizabeth or Elisabeth from the Hebrew meaning "God's promise, God is my oath". In the bible, Elizabeth was the mother of John the Baptist.

Ethan (M)

The name of a wise man in the Old Testament, this Hebrew name means "firm, enduring".

Eve (F)

According to the Bible, Eve was the first woman. Eve is derived from Hebrew and means "life".

Gabriella (F)

This is an Italian feminine form of Gabriel, which is a Hebrew name meaning "strong man of God". The name is derived from the Archangel Gabriel who in the Bible announces the birth of Jesus to Mary.

Hannah (F)

A Hebrew name meaning "God has favoured me". In the Old Testament Hannah is the mother of the prophet Samuel.

Isaiah (M)

This Hebrew name means "God is salvation" and was borne by a major prophet of the Old Testament.

Jacob (M)

Of Hebrew origin this name means "supplanter" – in the Bible Jacob tricks his older twin brother Esau out of his inheritance. The biblical Jacob fathered twelve sons who founded the twelve tribes of Israel.

James (M)

Of English origin, James is a variant of Jacob and as such means the same, i.e "he who supplants". The King James Bible is named in reference to James I of England (16th-17th century) who commissioned the translation into English of what has become the primary faith document of many Christians today.

Jeremiah (M)

This biblical name means "God will uplift" and is Hebrew in origin. Jeremiah is a major Old Testament prophet.

Jessica (F)

Of uncertain meaning, Jessica is probably derived from the Hebrew Old Testament name Jesca. The name Jessica appears to have been invented by Shakespeare (for Shylock's daughter in The Merchant of Venice).

Joel (M)

Of Hebrew origin, and its meaning is "Jehovah is the Lord"

John (M)

Of Hebrew origin, meaning "the Lord is gracious". The name of the longest-lived of the 12 apostles, who was especially loved by Christ. Also the name of John the Baptist, who baptized Christ in the Jordan river.

Jonathan (M)

A biblical name of Hebrew origin meaning "God has given".

Joseph (M)

This name is an English form of the Hebrew name Yosef, and means "God will increase". The name Joseph is borne by several major biblical figures including Joseph of Arimathea who took Jesus down from the cross and buried him.

Joshua (M)

Of Hebrew origin, and its meaning is "Jehovah is salvation".

Jude

This is a short form of Judas, taken from the Apostle Judas Thaddaeus, the patron saint of desperate cases. The meaning of the name Jude is derived from Hebrew and is "praised".

Judith (F)

A Hebrew name meaning "woman of Judea". In the Old Testament Judith was one of Esau's wives.

Leah (F)

It is of Hebrew origin, and its meaning is "delicate". Biblically, Leah was the name of Jacob's first wife.

Lilith (F)

Lilith was Adam's wife, before Eve, and was turned into a demon for disobeying him. Her name is of Assyrian origin and means "belonging to the night".

Lola (F)

A Spanish pet form of Dolores, meaning "sorrows". Dolores comes from the Spanish title for the Virgin Mary – **María de los Dolores** ("Mary of Sorrows").

Luke (M)

This biblical name is of Greek origin and means "man from Lucania" (a region in Italy). In the New Testament, Luke is a disciple of Jesus and a doctor. Luke is the patron saint of physicians and surgeons.

Madeleine (F)

A French form of Magdalene, meaning "woman of Magdala". It originates from Mary Magdalene, a figure in the New Testament, who hailed from the village of Magdala on Lake Galilee.

Mark (M)

Of Latin origin, meaning "dedicated to Mars", Mark was the writer of one of the gospels.

Martha (F)

A name of Aramaic origin meaning "lady". In the bible, she was the sister of Lazarus and Mary, and in the Gospel of John was witness to Jesus' resurrection of her brother.

Mary (F)

It is of Latin origin, and its meaning is "star of the sea". Saint Jerome associated the Virgin's name with the Latin phrase "stella maris". Other possible meanings are (Hebrew) "wished-for child" and "rebellion". In the bible, the virgin mother of Christ, Mary became the object of great veneration in the Catholic Church. Through the centuries, names like Dolores and Mercedes have been created to express aspects of Mary's life and worship.

Matthew (M)

Meaning "gift of God", this name is of Hebrew origin.

Mercedes (F)

Of Spanish origin, meaning "mercies". Used in reference to the Virgin Mary, Santa Maria de las Mercedes as "Our Lady of Mercies". Mercedes is the name of the lost love of Edmond Dantes in Dumas's **The Count of Monte Cristo**.

Michael (M)

Of Hebrew origin, meaning "who resembles God". In the Bible, Michael is an archangel who leads the army of heaven, and Saint Michael is the patron saint of soldiers.

Miguel (M)

A form of Michael, a Hebrew name meaning "who resembles God".

Nathaniel (M)

A biblical name of Hebrew origin meaning "God has given".

Nevaeh (F)

A modern name, "Nevaeh" is literally "heaven" written backwards.

Nicholas (M)

Of Greek origin, Nicholas means "victory of the people". Saint Nicholas is the patron saint of children.

Noah (M)

This name is of Hebrew origin and probably means "rest" or "comfort". In the Old Testament Noah builds an ark to save his family and a pair of every species of living thing from the Flood.

Peter (M)

A name of Greek origin meaning "stone" (or rock). Christ's disciple Peter is traditionally regarded by Christians as the metaphorical foundation stone of the Church, for Jesus says of Peter "upon this rock I will build my church".

Rachel (F)

A Hebrew name meaning "ewe". In the Bible it is the name of Jacob's favourite wife who is described as a beauty.

Rebekah (F)

The name Rebekah is a variant of Rebecca, the meaning of which is "to bind". In the book of Genesis the account of Rebekah is of a maiden of beauty, modesty, and kindness who became the wife of Abraham's son, Isaac.

Ruben (M)

A form of Reuben, which is a biblical name of Hebrew origin meaning "behold, a son". In the Old Testament, Reuben founds one of the twelve tribes of Israel.

Ruth (F)

It is of Hebrew origin, and its meaning is "friend, companion". In the bible Ruth was the young Moabite widow who said to her mother-in-law, "Where you go, there I shall go also; your people will be my people, your God, my God".

Samuel (M)

Meaning "God has heard" this name is of Hebrew origin. The biblical Samuel was a major Hebrew judge and prophet who established the Hebrew monarchy.

Sarah (F)

A biblical name meaning "princess". In the bible, Sarah, originally called Sarai, shared anomadic life with her husband Abraham. She is described as being exceptionally beautiful even into her older years.

Sebastian (M)

This name means "man from Sebaste" being derived from a Roman Christian martyr who came from Sebaste, a town in Asia Minor. "Sebaste" comes from the Greek word for "venerable".

Stephen (M)

Meaning "crown", this name is of Greek origin. Saint Stephen is regarded as the first Christian martyr, and is remembered in the Western Christian calendar on 26 December, St Stephen's Day.

Tabitha (F)

Meaning "gazelle", this biblical name is of Aramaic origin.

Thomas (M)

This name is derived from Greek and Aramaic and means "twin". In the New Testament Thomas is a disciple of Jesus who is initially reluctant to accept Christ's resurrection, hence the phrase 'doubting Thomas'.

Tobias (M)

Of Hebrew origin, Tobias means "the Lord is good".

Toby (M)

Of English origin, short form of Tobias, meaning "the Lord is good".

Zachary (M)

This name means "God remembers", and is derived from the Hebrew name Zechariah, a name borne by an Old Testament prophet.

Ace (M)
Originally an English nickname, Ace means "the best, number one".

Aidan (M)
It is of Gaelic origin, meaning "fire".

Alexander (M)
Meaning "man's defender and helper" this name is Greek in origin. A famous bearer of this name was Alexander the Great, who in the fourth century BC conquered most of the known world.

Alexis (F)
Greek in origin, this name is derived from the male name "Alexius" and means "defender" or "helper".

Alfie (M)
This is a pet form of the Old English name Alfred, and has latterly become a given name in its own right. Alfred means "elf counsel".

Alice (F)
Of Old German origin, meaning "noble, exalted". Made famous by the heroine in Lewis Carroll's "Alice's Adventures in Wonderland" (1865) and "Through the Looking Glass" (1872), who was based on his child friend Alice Lidell, daughter of the Dean of Christ Church, Oxford.

Alison (F)
Of Old German origin, meaning "noble, exalted".

Amber (F)
From Arabic "ambar". Amber is the English name for a semiprecious gem also used to describe the golden colour. In Hindi, the name is derived from Sanskrit, meaning "the sky".

Amelia (F)
Of Latin and Old German origin, meaning "industrious; striving".

Amy (F)
Of Latin origin, Amy means "beloved" and is an English version of the Old French name Amée.

Angharad (F)
Borne by a figure in Welsh mythology, and associated with Welsh royalty, this name means "much loved".

Anne (F)
A variant of Ann (Hebrew) meaning "favoured grace".

Antonio (M)
A Spanish and Italian form of Anthony.

Antony (M)
Derived from the ancient Roman family name of Antonius (a famous member of which was the general Mark Antony). The meaning of Antonio is unclear, however it is associated with goodness, being the name of a third century saint who founded Christian monasticism.

Anya (F)
This Russian name is a diminutive of Anna, and means "grace".

Asa (M)
A Hebrew name meaning "healer, doctor".

Ashanti (F)

A name of Ghanaian origin. Adopted from the name of the Ashanti people and region, and the once powerful Ghanaian Empire of Ashanti where traditionally women exercised great influence.

Ava (F)

There are several meanings and sources for this name. Ava means "voice, sound" in Persian. It may be a variant of Eve, or be derived from a Germanic name and mean "desired". It could also be interpreted as meaning "bird" from the Latin word avis.

Beatrix (F)

Derived from Latin and meaning "to make happy".

Beau (M)

A French name meaning "handsome". It was originally used as a nickname (famously borne by the English Regency dandy "Beau"[George Bryan] Brummell), before being adopted as a proper name. The profile of this name was raised by the hero of the novel Beau Geste (1924) and the character of Beau Wilks in the 1930s book and film Gone with the Wind.

Bethany (F)

Bethany was the name of a village near Jerusalem where Jesus visited with Mary, Martha and Lazarus. Popular with Roman Catholics.

Blair (M)

A Scottish name taken from the Gaelic word for "plain, field".

Blythe (F)

A name of Old English origin meaning "carefree" and "cheerful".

Bradley (M)

Of Old English origin, meaning "broad meadow".

Bran (M)

This name means "raven" in Welsh and Irish Gaelic.

Brandon (M)
Of Old English origin, meaning "broom [shrub], gorse hill". Variant of the less popular Brendon.

Brianna (F)
Meaning "virtuous; strong", Brianna is a feminine form of the Irish name Brian.

Brice
From Welsh origins and meaning "speckled".

Caitlin (F)
A Gaelic form of Katharine, meaning "pure".

Callum (M)
This is a Gaelic form of the Latin name Columba, meaning "dove", the symbol of peace and gentleness. Saint Columba was a sixth-century Irish missionary who was behind Scotland's conversion to Christianity.

Cameron (M)
A Gaelic name meaning "crooked nose", adopted from the surname of the Scottish Cameron clan.

Candida (F)
Latin in origin this name means "white".

Carl (M)
A name of Germanic origin meaning "free man".

Carys (F)
A Welsh name meaning "love".

Cato (M)
This name dates back to Ancient Roman times and its Latin meaning is "wise".

Charles (M)

Of Old German origin, meaning "free man". Charles and its variant forms have been favoured by the royalty of several countries for several centuries, including the present Prince of Wales.

Charlotte (F)

A French name meaning "little woman" – a pet form of the name Charles.

Conner (M)

Of Gaelic origin, meaning "hound-lover". The name of a legendary king of Ulster who lived at the time of Christ.

Courtney (F)

An aristocratic English surname which latterly has been adopted as a given name. The original surname may take its source from the place-name Courtenay in Northern France, or Courtney may be derived from the Old French court nez meaning "short nose".

Dakota (F)

A Native American name meaning "friend".

Dale (M)

An adoption of an English surname borne originally by people who lived near a dale or valley.

Daniel (M)

Of Hebrew origin, meaning "God is my judge". In the old Testament, Daniel was a Hebrew prophet living in Babylon where he served in the court of the king, interpreting his dreams. He was persecuted for his faith in God, which kept him alive in a den of lions.

Danielle (F)
Of Hebrew and French origin, meaning "God is my Judge". Feminine variant of Daniel.

Darcy (F)
Of French origin derived from the surname of the aristocratic "d'Arcy" family who settled in Ireland in the fourteenth century.

Darragh (M)
This name means "oak" and is derived from Gaelic.

David (M)
Of Hebrew origin, meaning "beloved". In the bible, David was a shepherd and writer of Psalms. St David is the patron saint of Wales.

Deborah (F)
A Hebrew name meaning "bee". In the bible Deborah was a prophetess who summoned Barak to battle against an invading army.

Declan (M)
Of Irish origin, the name of an Irish 6th century saint

Delaney (M)
A name of Gaelic origin meaning "challenger".

Delilah (F)
Of Hebrew origin, meaning "languishing, lovelorn, seductive". In the bible, Delilah was the woman who beguiled Samson into revealing the secret of his superhuman strength.

Dexter (M)
An adopted occupational surname which means "dyer" in Old English, although Dexter is probably known better for its co-incidental Latin meaning of "skillful, right-handed".

Dominic (M)

Of Latin derivation, Dominic means "of the Lord" and traditionally it was bestowed on children born on a Sunday.

Douglas (M)

A name of Gaelic origin (from a Scottish clan name), meaning "dark stream".

Dylan (M)

Of Welsh origin, meaning "son of the sea". In Welsh mythology Dylan is the son of the virgin goddess Aranrhod. It is also the name of one of Wales most famous sons, Dylan Thomas.

Earl (M)

An ancient English title for noblemen which carries the meaning of "nobleman" and "warrior".

Ebele (F)

An African name meaning "merciful, kind".

Ebrel (F)

A Cornish name meaning the month of April.

Edward (M)

This name originates from Old English and means "prosperous defender".

Elijah (M)

A Hebrew name which means "Yahweh is God".

Elizabeth (F)

Elizabeth or Elisabeth from the Hebrew meaning "God's promise, God is my oath". In the bible, Elizabeth was the mother of John the Baptist.

Ella (F)

Meaning "bright light" is a popular name in all English speaking countries, regularly making the 'top names' lists and is also popular in Norwegian and Swedish speaking countries.

Ellie (F)
Ellie means "sun ray; bright light" and is of Old German and Greek origin.

Ellis (M)
Of English origin, anglicization of Elias, from Elijah.

Emer (F)
In Irish legend Emer was the accomplished wife of Cuchulainn, possessing beauty, eloquence and wisdom. Of Gaelic origin, the meaning is uncertain, possibly "swift" or "twin".

Emilio (M)
This name means "rival" and is derived from the Roman family name "Aemilius".

Emily (F)
This is the femine of Emilio and as such means the same, i.e "rival". It is derived from the Roman family name "Aemilius".

Emma (F)
It is of Old French and Old German origin, and its meaning is "entire or universal".

Eric (M)
Of Scandinavian origin, this name means "forever ruler" or "one ruler".

Erin (F)
Meaning "Ireland", derived from "Eire", the Gaelic word for Ireland.

Euan (M)

Of Irish and Gaelic origin, meaning "little swift one". Also possibly from Eoghan, a Gaelic name meaning "youth".

Evander (M)

Borne by a hero in Roman mythology, Evander is a name of Greek origin and means "good man".

Evie (F)

The girl's name is a variant of Evelyn, meaning "life, animal".

Faith (F)

An English "virtue name" particularly associated with trust and belief in God.

Fallon (F)

An Irish name meaning "leader". Fallon is derived from the Gaelic surname Ó Fallamhain.

Felicity (F)

An English name meaning "happiness".

Felix (M)

This name means "lucky, joyful" in Latin.

Finlay (M)

From the Gaelic name Fionnlagh, meaning "fair warrior".

Fiona (F)

Derived from the Gaelic word "fionn" this name means "white", "fair".

Ford (M)

Adopted from the English surname, meaning "ford", as in a point where a river can be crossed on foot.

Fred (M)

A variant of Alfred (Old English) and Frederick (Old German), and the meaning of Fred is "elf or magical counsel".

Frederick (M)

Meaning "peaceful ruler", this name is Germanic in origin.

Gabriella (F)

This is an Italian feminine form of Gabriel, which is a Hebrew name meaning "strong man of God". The name is derived from the Archangel Gabriel who in the Bible announces the birth of Jesus to Mary.

Galen (M)

This is a name of Greek origin meaning "calm". This name is closely associated with Claudius Galenus a second century BC physician whose writings furthered medical knowledge.

Geneviève (F)

A French name of Celtic origin which probably means "woman of the people". A famous namesake was Saint Geneviève, the patron saint of Paris, who roused the city to resist a Hun attack in the fifth century.

George (M)

This name means "farmer, to work the earth", and is Greek in origin. It has been a popular name with British royalty since the eighteenth century and George III, was known as "Farmer George" for his interest in agriculture.

Georgia (F)

Of Greek origin, this is the feminine form of George.

Gerard (M)

This Germanic name means "spear brave".

Geronimo (M)

An Italian form of Jerome, a name of Greek origin meaning "sacred name". Geronimo was the name bestowed upon the celebrated Apache warrior chief, Goyathlay (1829-1909).

Giada (F)

An Italian name meaning "jade".

Giselle (F)

A French name meaning "pledge". Giselle is popularly associated in English-speaking countries with the ballet of the same name.

Gita (F)

Meaning "song", this is an Indian name of Sanskrit origin.

Grace (F)

An English "virtue name" meaning "grace", in the sense of "the grace of God". To modern ears "Grace" is also suggestive of gracious manners and elegance.

Hari

This is one of the names of the Hindu god Vishnu. There are several meanings attached to this name including "brown, tawny, monkey, lion".

Harrison (M)

Of Old English origin, meaning "son of Harry".

Harry (M)

Used as a nickname of Henry and Harold, of Old German origin meaning "home ruler". Fictional character Harry Potter has also influenced the name and Prince Henry of Wales is widely known as Harry.

Harvey (M)

Of Old English and Old French origin, meaning "eager for battle; strong and worthy".

Heidi (F)

Meaning "noble", Heidi is a short form of the German name "Adelheid" (Adelaide in English). Heidi is the title, and central character of the much loved children's classic novel set in the Swiss Alps written by Johanna Spyri in 1880.

Henrietta (F)

A feminine form of Henry, a name of Germanic origin which means "home-ruler".

Holly (F)

An English name from the evergreen holly shrub or tree. Holly sprigs are traditionally used as Christmas decorations and so this name is particularly associated with girls born around Christmas.

Hope (F)

An English "virtue name" traditionally denoting a Christian hope for eternal life. In modern times this name has become associated with "optimism".

Hugo (M)

Of Germanic origin, the meaning of Hugo is "heart, mind, spirit".

Ignatius (M)

This Latin name, derived from the old Roman family name of Egnatius, means "fire".

Imogen (F)

Meaning "maiden", Imogen is the name of a princess in Shakespeare's play **Cymbeline**. It is a name of Gaelic origin and is derived from the figure of Innogen, from Celtic legend.

Isaac (M)

A Hebrew name meaning "he laughs".

Isadora (F)

This name means "gift of Isis", and is derived from Greek.

Isabella (F)
Of Spanish and Latin origin, a variant of Elizabeth from the Hebrew meaning "God's promise, God is my oath".

Isaiah (M)
This Hebrew name means "God is salvation" and was borne by a major prophet of the Old Testament.

Isla (F)
A Scottish name meaning "from Islay" – the name of a Hebridean island.

Jack (M)
This has evolved from a medieval English pet name for John. So the meaning of Jack is linked to that of the Hebrew name John, which is "God is gracious".

Jacob (M)
Of Hebrew origin this name means "supplanter" – in the Bible Jacob tricks his older twin brother Esau out of his inheritance. The biblical Jacob fathered twelve sons who founded the twelve tribes of Israel.

Jake (M)
This English name developed in the Middle Ages as a version of Jack , but is now used as a given name in its own right. Also, Jake can be used as a pet form of Jacob.

James (M)
Of English origin, James is a variant of Jacob and as such means the same, i.e "he who supplants". The King James Bible is named in reference to James I of England (16th-17th century) who commissioned the translation into English of what has become the primary faith document of many Christians today.

Jay (M)
This is an Indian name derived from Sanskrit and meaning "victory".

Jennifer (F)

A Cornish form of Guinevere (King Arthur's wife of Celtic legend), and means "fair; white; smooth".

Jeremiah (M)

This biblical name means "God will uplift" and is Hebrew in origin. Jeremiah is a major Old Testament prophet.

Jett (M)

Denoting a deep black colour from the English word "jet".

Jody (F)

Originally a nickname of Judith, meaning "from Judea".

Joel (M)

Of Hebrew origin, and its meaning is "Jehovah is the Lord"

Joseph (M)

This name is an English form of the Hebrew name Yosef, and means "God will increase". The name Joseph is borne by several major biblical figures including Joseph of Arimathea who took Jesus down from the cross and buried him.

Julian (M)

Of Greek origin, meaning "Jove's child". Variant of Julius, the family clan name of several of the most powerful Roman emperors.

Juliet (F)

Of Latin origin, meaning "youthful; Jove's child". diminutive of Julia, feminine form of Julian. Possibly Shakespeare's most well known heroine, from **Romeo and Juliet.**

Kaden (M)

A name of multiple meanings. Firstly, "companion" from Arabic, secondly it can be linked to a German surname meaning "fen" as in marshy land. It also has the meaning of "fighter" derived from an Irish Gaelic surname.

Kaimana (M)
This is a Hawaiian name meaning "power of the ocean". It can also be taken to mean "diamond" as it is the Hawaiian transcription of that word.

Kalinda
An Indian name meaning "the sun".

Kallista (F)
This is a Greek name meaning "beautiful".

Kalyan (M)
This Indian name means "lovely, auspicious" in Sanskrit.

Katherine (F)
From the word "katharos" meaning "pure" in Greek.

Keely (F)
A name of Gaelic origin meaning "slender".

Keira
A variant of Kyra (Greek), meaning "lady".

Kent (M)
It is of Old English origin, and its meaning is "edge".

Kerenza (F)
A Cornish name meaning "love".

Kevin (M)
Meaning "handsome, beloved", this name is an Anglicized form of the Irish Gaelic name Caoimhin.

Khalid (M)
A name of Arabic origin meaning "eternal".

Kieran (M)
Meaning "black", this name is an Anglicized form of the Irish Gaelic name Ciarán.

Kizziah
This African name means "favourite".

Kim (F)
A short form of Kimberley, an English surname adopted as a given name. Kim is also a Vietnamese name meaning "golden".

Kofi (M)
This African name means "born on a Friday".

Kurt (M)
A short form of the Germanic name Conrad, meaning "bold advice".

Kyle (M)
Of Gaelic origin, meaning "narrow, straight".

Laetitia (F)
Latin in origin this name means "joy".

Lalita (F)
An Indian name of Sanskrit origin meaning "playful" and "charming". In Hindu mythology Lalita is a playmate of the young Krishna.

Lauren (F)
An English name derived from the Latin word for "laurel".

Layla (F)
An Arabic name meaning "night". Made popular by the song of the same name by Eric Clapton.

Leilani (F)

It is of Hawaiian origin, and means "heavenly lei or royal child of heaven".

Leo (M)

Of Latin origin, and its meaning is "lion".

Leona (F)

Meaning "like a lion" this name is of Latin origin.

Levi (M)

Of Hebrew origin, meaning "joined".

Lewis (M)

Anglicization of Louis (Old German, French) meaning "renowned fighter".

Liam (M)

This is an Irish short form of William, a name of Germanic origin which can be interpreted as meaning "strong protector".

Lisa (F)

Of English origin, it is a short form of Elizabeth meaning "God's promise".

Liv (F)

Meaning "protection" this name is derived from Old Norse. "Liv" is also a modern Scandinavian word for "life".

Llewellyn (M)

This Welsh name could have arisen from two ancient Celtic sun deities, Lug and Belenus, and mean "shining". It could also mean "like a lion" (from the Welsh word for lion, llew.)

Logan (M)

Adopted from the Scottish surname, this name means "little hollow" and takes it source from a Scottish place-name.

Lola (F)

A Spanish pet form of Dolores, meaning "sorrows". Dolores comes from the Spanish title for the Virgin Mary – María de los Dolores ("Mary of Sorrows").

Louis (M)
Meaning "famous warrior", this name is of French and Germanic origin, and has been borne by many French kings.

Lucy (F)
Derived from Latin and meaning "light".

Luke (M)
This biblical name is of Greek origin and means "man from Lucania" (a region in Italy). In the New Testament, Luke is a disciple of Jesus and a doctor. Luke is the patron saint of physicians and surgeons.

Mabel (F)
Of English origin, meaning is "lovable".

Madeleine (F)
A French form of Magdalene, meaning "woman of Magdala". It originates from Mary Magdalene, a figure in the New Testament, who hailed from the village of Magdala on Lake Galilee.

Madison (F)
Of Old English origin, meaning "son of the mighty warrior".

Maisie (F)
A nickname for Margaret of Old English origin, meaning "pearl".

Malika (F)
This is an Arabic name meaning "queen". Malika is also a Hungarian name meaning "hard-working".

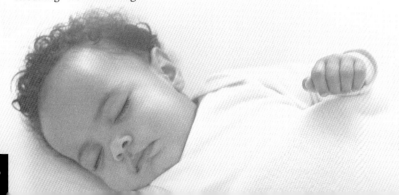

Malina (F)
A Polish, Czech and Slovak name meaning "raspberry".

Malory (F)
Meaning "unfortunate", this name comes from an English surname of Norman origin.

Marcus (M)
Of Latin origin, meaning "dedicated to Mars". Mars being the Roman god of fertility.

Mark (M)
Of Latin origin, meaning "dedicated to Mars", Mark was the writer of one of the gospels.

Matilda (F)
Meaning "strong fighter", this name is of Germanic origin.

Maverick (M)
This name means "independent" and "unorthodox person". It is adopted from the surname of a nineteenth-century Texas rancher who defied convention by not branding his calves. Thus "maverick" passed into common parlance as a title for unconventional behaviour.

Max (M)
Meaning "greatest", this Latin name is derived from an ancient Roman family name.

May (F)
Literally a month name; "May". May is also an English word for the hawthorn flower which blossoms in May.

Megan (F)
Of Welsh origin, this name is a popular variant of Margaret meaning "pearl".

Melanie (F)
Meaning "black, dark" this name is derived from Greek.

Mercedes (F)
Of Spanish origin, meaning "mercies". Used in reference to the Virgin Mary, Santa Maria de las Mercedes as "Our Lady of Mercies". It is the name of the lost love of Edmond Dantes in Dumas's The Count of Monte Cristo.

Meredith (F)
From an old Welsh name "Maredudd" which possibly means "great Lord". Originally a boy's name it is now regarded as girl's name.

Mia (F)
An Italian name meaning "mine".

Michael (M)
Of Hebrew origin, meaning "who resembles God". In the Bible, Michael is an archangel who leads the army of heaven, and Saint Michael is the patron saint of soldiers.

Miguel (M)
A form of Michael, a Hebrew name meaning "who resembles God".

Miles (M)
From the Old German "merciful; eager to please".

Milo (M)
The meaning of Milo is uncertain though it may be connected to a Slavic word meaning "gracious".

Miranda (F)
From Latin, meaning "admirable, wonderful". This name was invented by Shakespeare for the heroine of his play The Tempest.

Mohammed (M)
Arabic, meaning "praiseworthy".

Molly (F)
Of Irish origin, a nickname of Mary (Latin) "star of the sea". In use since the late Middle Ages. In the past, it has had negative connotations, given that "moll" means a prostitute or a gangster's girlfriend.

Montgomery (M)

This name is taken from an English surname, of Norman origin, which translates as "Gomeric's mountain" (Gomeric is a Germanic name meaning "power of man"). A distinguished bearer of this surname was the British Field Marshal Bernard Montgomery.

Morven

A Scottish unisex name taken from a Gaelic place-name meaning "big peak". Morven is also a mythical Scots kingdom.

Nasrin (F)

A Persian name meaning "wild rose".

Natalie (F)

Of Latin origin, meaning "birthday".

Natasha (F)

Of Russian origin, a variant of Natalie.

Niall (M)

The meaning of this Gaelic name is uncertain. Some interpretations are "champion", "passionate" and "cloud".

Niamh (F)

An Irish name meaning "bright". Niamh was the daughter of the sea god in Irish legend.

Nicholas (M)

Of Greek origin, Nicholas means "victory of the people". Saint Nicholas is the patron saint of children.

Noah (M)

This name is of Hebrew origin and probably means "rest" or "comfort". In the Old Testament Noah builds an ark to save his family and a pair of every species of living thing from the Flood.

Nye (M)
This is a short form of the Welsh name Aneurin. Its meaning is uncertain although it is possibly "noble".

Oceana
A name of Greek origin meaning "ocean".

Oliver (M)
Of Latin origin, meaning "olive tree", the title character in the book by Charles Dickens.

Olivia (F)
Derived from the Latin word for "olive".

Omorose (F)
An African name meaning "beautiful".

Orlando (M)
This is an Italian form of Roland, a Germanic name meaning "famous land".

Oscar (M)
This name may be of Scandinavian origin and be associated with divinity, meaning "god spear". It could also be derived from Gaelic and mean "deer-lover". In Irish legend, Oscar was the grandson of the hero Fionn mac Cumhail.

Owain (M)
A Welsh name meaning "well-bred." An illustrious bearer of this name was the medieval Welsh national hero Owain Glyndwr.

Owen (M)
Of Welsh and Greek origin, meaning "well-born, noble".

Paige (F)
Adopted from the English occupational surname meaning young servant to a lord.

Patricia (F)

Meaning "noble woman", Patricia takes its source from the Roman name Patricius.

Penelope (F)

A name of uncertain origin and obscure meaning. In Greek mythology Penelope's husband Odysseus leaves her for twenty years to fight in the Trojan War. During that time Penelope was assumed to be a widow and was besieged by numerous suitors, all of whom she manages to rebut through trickery. Hence the name Penelope is associated with cunning, patience and fidelity.

Peregrine (M)

Latin in origin, this name carries the meanings of "sojourner" and "stranger".

Phoebe (F)

This name means "bright", and is of Greek origin.

Piers (M)

Of Greek origin, meaning "rock". Peter is the Latin form of the name that the Normans brought to Britain as Piers.

Pip (M)

This is a short form of Philip, a Greek name meaning "horse-lover". The name Pip is associated with the endearing fictional character from Charles Dickens's novel Great Expectations (1861).

Portia (F)

Derived from the Roman family name Porcius. Portia is a character of great eloquence in Shakespeare's **The Merchant of Venice**.

Primo (M)

This name means "first" and is of Latin origin.

Qamar (M)

An Arabic name meaning "moon".

Quincy

Adopted from the English surname Quincy, itself derived from a Latin personal name, Quintus, meaning "fifth".

Quinn (M)

This name means "chief" and is derived from an Irish Gaelic surname.

Quy

This Vietnamese unisex name means "precious".

Rachel (F)

A Hebrew name meaning "ewe". In the Bible it is the name of Jacob's favourite wife who is described as a beauty.

Randolph (M)

Derived from Old Norse this name means "shield wolf", which can be interpreted as denoting a formidable protector.

Rebekah (F)

The name Rebekah is a variant of Rebecca, the meaning of which is "to bind". In the book of Genesis the account of Rebekah is of a maiden of beauty, modesty, and kindness who became the wife of Abraham's son, Isaac.

Reece (M)

This name means "enthusiastic" and is an Anglicized form of the Welsh name Rhys.

Regan (F)
An Irish name meaning "queenly".

Rex (M)
This is a Latin name meaning "king".

Rhianna (F)
A Welsh name meaning "great queen" or "goddess". Rhianna is a form of Rhiannon, who is the goddess of fertility and the moon in Welsh mythology.

Rhys (M)
Of Welsh origin, meaning "enthusiasm". Native Welsh form of Reece.

Richard (M)
Of Old German origin, meaning "powerful leader".

Riordan (M)
This Irish name means "royal poet".

Robert (M)
A name of Germanic origin meaning "bright; renowned".

Roxanne (F)
It is of Persian origin, and means "dawn".

Roxy (F)
An English pet form of Roxana, which is a name of Persian origin, meaning "dawn" or "bright".

Ruben (M)
A form of Reuben, which is a biblical name of Hebrew origin meaning "behold, a son". In the Old Testament, Reuben founds one of the twelve tribes of Israel.

Rufus (M)
This name means "red-haired" in Latin.

Ryan (M)
It is of Gaelic origin, meaning "king".

Salvador (M)
This Spanish name means "saviour" and is derived from Latin.

Saoirse (F)
This Irish Gaelic name means "freedom".

Sasha
The Russian pet name for Alexander, which has been adopted as a proper name for both boys and girls.

Scarlett (F)
Meaning "red, scarlet" this name was popularized by the fictional heroine Scarlett O'Hara from the 1930s book and film **Gone with the Wind**. It comes from an English occupational surname (derived from Old French) for someone who dyed or sold rich, bright cloth.

Scott (M)
Meaning Scot "from Scotland, a Scotsman".

Sean (M)
It is of Irish origin, a variant of John (Hebrew) meaning "the Lord is gracious".

Sebastian (M)
This name means "man from Sebaste" being derived from a Roman Christian martyr who came from Sebaste, a town in Asia Minor. "Sebaste" comes from the Greek word for "venerable".

Serena (F)
A Latin name meaning "serene, calm".

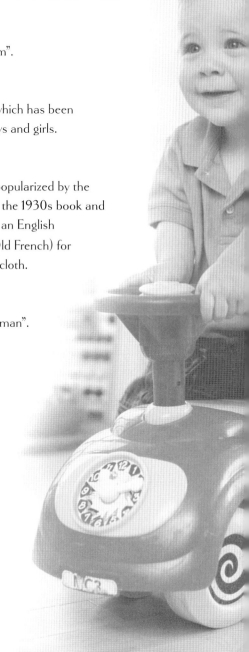

Skye (F)
A Scottish place-name – the Isle of Skye off Scotland's west coast. Also a form of the English name "Sky", meaning literally "sky".

Sophia (F)
Meaning "wisdom", from Greek origins. A variant of Sophie.

Stella (F)
From Latin, meaning "star".

Stephen (M)
Meaning "crown", this name is of Greek origin. Saint Stephen is regarded as the first Christian martyr, and is remembered in the Western Christian calendar on 26 December, St Stephen's Day.

Sterling (M)
This name comes from Old English and means "little star".

Stuart (M)
Of Old English origin, meaning "steward".

Tabitha (F)
Meaning "gazelle", this biblical name is of Aramaic origin.

Tallulah (F)
This is a Native American name meaning "leaping water".

Tamar (F)
A Hebrew name meaning "palm tree".

Tane (M)
A Maori name meaning "man". In Polynesian mythology Tane is the god of forests, and according to legend he created the first man.

Tasi

Meaning "sea, ocean" in the Chamorro language of Guam, Micronesia.

Tatum (F)

Of Old English origin, from a surname meaning "Tata's homestead". It could also carry the meaning of "cheerful".

Thomas (M)

This name is derived from Greek and Aramaic and means "twin". In the New Testament Thomas is a disciple of Jesus who is initially reluctant to accept Christ's resurrection.

Tim (M)

A variant of Timothy (Greek), meaning "God's honor".

Tito (M)

This name can be traced to an ancient Roman name and probably means "title of honour".

Tobias (M)

Of Hebrew origin, Tobias means "the Lord is good".

Toby (M)

Of English origin, short form of Tobias, meaning "the Lord is good".

Ulani

A Hawaiian name meaning "happy".

Ulrika (F)

This Scandinavian name means "wealthy leader".

Ume (F)

A Japanese name meaning "plum blossom", a symbol of devotion in Japanese culture.

Umi (M)

Meaning "life", this name is of African origin.

Valentine (M)
Meaning "strong, healthy" this name is derived from an old Roman family name.

Vance (M)
This is from a surname meaning "marshland" and is of Old English origin.

Victoria (F)
From Latin origins, this name means "victory".

Ward (M)
This name means "guardian", being taken from the Old English occupational surname for a guardian or watchman.

Winona (F)
A Native American name for a firstborn daughter.

Wyatt (M)
A combative name which takes its source from an Old English name (Wigheard), which translates as "war" and "hardy, brave".

Wyclif (M)
Adopted from an English surname, this name means "white cliff".

Xanthe (F)
This name comes from Greek and means "bright; yellow".

Xavier (M)
This probably means "the new house" from a Basque place name. It is also a name of Arabic origin and means "bright, splendid".

Xuan (M)
A Vietnamese name meaning "spring".

Xylia (F)
This name means "of the forest" or "woods-dweller" and is derived from Greek.

Yani (F)
An Australian Aboriginal name meaning "peace".

Yash (M)
Meaning "glory, fame", this Indian name is derived from Sanskrit.

Yi (M)
This is a Chinese given name of multiple meanings, one of which is "justice".

Yves (M)
Meaning "yew", this is a French name of Germanic origin.

Zachary (M)
This name means "God remembers", and is derived from the Hebrew name Zechariah, a name borne by an Old Testament prophet.

Zara (F)
Of Arabic origin, meaning "radiance".

Zayn (M)
An Arabic name meaning "beauty, grace".

Zlatan (M)
A Slavic name meaning "gold" or "golden".

Zoe (F)
A Greek name meaning "life".

Beau (M)

A French name meaning "handsome". It was originally used as a nickname (famously borne by the English Regency dandy "Beau"[George Bryan] Brummell), before being adopted as a proper name. The profile of this name was raised by the hero of the novel Beau Geste (1924) and the character of Beau Wilks in the 1930s book and film **Gone with the Wind**.

Brontë (F)

Taken from the surname of the literary Brontë sisters, this name has Greek origins and means "thunder".

Dante

This is a name of Latin origin meaning "enduring". An impressive namesake was Italian poet Dante Alighieri (1265-1321), the author of **The Divine Comedy**.

Demelza (F)

Taken from the Cornish place-name of Demelza which means "fortified". Demelza has only been recorded as a first name from about the middle of the twentieth century. The name probably owes its heightened profile to the heroine of Winston Graham's Cornish "Poldark" novels.

Elanor (F)

A literary invention – borne by a character in J.R.R. Tolkien's The Lord of The Rings.
Elanor means "sun-star" in the author's invented Elvish language.

Haydn

After the great composer Josef Haydn (1732-1809).

Heidi (F)

Meaning "noble", Heidi is a short form of the German name "Adelheid" (Adelaide in English). Heidi is the title, and central character of the much loved children's classic novel set in the Swiss Alps written by Johanna Spyri in 1880.

Imogen (F)

Meaning "maiden", Imogen is the name of a princess in Shakespeare's play Cymbeline. It is a name of Gaelic origin and is derived from the figure of Innogen, from Celtic legend.

Jessica (F)

Of uncertain meaning, Jessica is probably derived from the Hebrew Old Testament name Jesca. The name Jessica appears to have been invented by Shakespeare (for Shylock's daughter in **The Merchant of Venice**).

Juliet (F)

Of Latin origin, meaning "youthful; Jove's child". diminutive of Julia, feminine form of Julian. Possibly Shakespeare's most well known heroine, from **Romeo and Juliet**.

Layla (F)

An Arabic name meaning "night". Made popular by the song of the same name by Eric Clapton.

Mercedes (F)

Of Spanish origin, meaning "mercies". Used in reference to the Virgin Mary, Santa Maria de las Mercedes as "Our Lady of Mercies". Mercedes is the name of the lost love of Edmond Dantes in Dumas's **The Count of Monte Cristo**.

Miranda (F)

From Latin, meaning "admirable, wonderful". This name was invented by Shakespeare for the heroine of his play **The Tempest**.

Pip (M)

This is a short form of Philip, a Greek name meaning "horse-lover". The name Pip is associated with the endearing fictional character from Charles Dickens's novel Great Expectations (1861).

Portia (F)

Derived from the Roman family name Porcius. Portia is a character of great eloquence in Shakespeare's **The Merchant of Venice.**

Scarlett (F)

Meaning "red, scarlet" this name was popularized by the fictional heroine Scarlett O'Hara from the 1930s book and film Gone with the Wind. It comes from an English occupational surname (derived from Old French) for someone who dyed or sold rich, bright cloth.

Wendy (F)

An English name meaning "friendly". It is believed that the name Wendy was invented by J.M. Barrie for a character in Peter Pan (1904). Apparently Barrie developed it from an authentic childish nickname "Fwendy-Wendy".

Angharad (F)

Borne by a figure in Welsh mythology, and associated with Welsh royalty, this name means "much loved".

Arthur (M)

Of Celtic origin, King Arthur and his Round Table of knights have become legendary figures. Latin form Artorius, meaning noble and courageous.

Chloe (F)

A Greek name meaning "green shoot". In Greek mythology Chloe is an epithet for the harvest goddess Demeter, and so the name Chloe is associated with plants.

Diana (F)

In Roman mythology Diana was the goddess of the moon and hunting. Her name means "divine".

Dylan (M)

Of Welsh origin, meaning "son of the sea". In Welsh mythology Dylan is the son of the virgin goddess Aranrhod. It is also the name of one of Wales most famous sons, Dylan Thomas.

Evander (M)

Borne by a hero in Roman mythology, Evander is a name of Greek origin and means "good man".

Freya (F)

In Norse mythology Freya is the goddess of love and beauty. Her name means "lady".

Imogen (F)

Meaning "maiden", Imogen is the name of a princess in Shakespeare's play Cymbeline. It is a name of Gaelic origin and is derived from the figure of Innogen, from Celtic legend.

Iris (F)

Means "rainbow" in Greek. In Greek mythology Iris was a goddess associated with the rainbow who acted as a messenger for the gods. Also a plant genus covering several hundred species.

Jacinta (F)

The Spanish form of Hyancinth, a name derived from the Greek mythological figure of Hyakinthos, from whose blood the flower was said to spring.

Jennifer (F)

A Cornish form of Guinevere (King Arthur's wife of Celtic legend), and means "fair; white; smooth".

Morven

A Scottish unisex name taken from a Gaelic place-name meaning "big peak". Morven is also a mythical Scots kingdom.

Niamh (F)

An Irish name meaning "bright". Niamh was the daughter of the sea god in Irish legend.

Oceana

A name of Greek origin meaning "ocean".

Penelope (F)

A name of uncertain origin and obscure meaning. In Greek mythology Penelope's husband Odysseus leaves her for twenty years to fight in the Trojan War. During that time Penelope was assumed to be a widow and was besieged by numerous suitors, all of whom she manages to rebut through trickery. Hence the name Penelope is associated with cunning, patience and fidelity.

Rhianna (F)

A Welsh name meaning "great queen" or "goddess". Rhianna is a form of Rhiannon, who is the goddess of fertility and the moon in Welsh mythology.

Silas (M)

A short form of Silvanus, a Latin name meaning "wood, forest". In Roman mythology Silvanus was the god of forests.

Tor (M)

A Scandinavian name meaning "thunder". This name comes from Thor, the Old Norse god of thunder and war.

Tristan (M)

In Celtic legend Tristan is a hero involved in a tragic love affair with an Irish princess Isolde. The name Tristan is of uncertain Celtic origin and meaning. It is sometimes mistakenly linked to the Latin word tristis, meaning "sad".

Ulysses (M)

A Latin form of Odysseus, a name borne by the legendary Greek hero of Homer's Odyssey who fought in the Trojan War. The meaning of the name is uncertain.

Venus (F)

Named after the Roman goddess of love and beauty.

Acacia (F)

It is of Greek origin, and means "thorny tree". It is the name of the flower related to the mimosa. In the bible, acacia wood was used to build the Arc of the Covenant.

Aidan (M)

It is of Gaelic origin, meaning "fire".

Alyssa (F)

From the herbaceous plant alyssum, which are beautiful, delicate plants that come in a variety of colours, most typically yellow or white.

Amaryllis (F)

It is of Greek origin, and its meaning is "fresh, sparkling" in addition to being a beautiful flower.

Amber (F)

From Arabic "ambar". Amber is the English name for a semiprecious gem also used to describe the golden colour. In Hindi, the name is derived from Sanskrit, meaning "the sky".

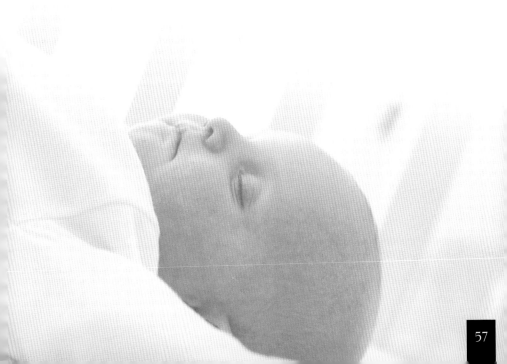

Anemone (F)

From Greek mythology, Anemone is the name of a nymph who was turned into a flower.

April (F)

It is of Latin origin, and its meaning is "to open". The month as a given name is often used to symbolize spring, and is therefore popular, along with May, for spring births - the time when buds open and flowers appear.

Ayanna (F)

It is of Kiswahili origin, and its meaning is "beautiful flower".

Bailey

From the English occupational surname "Bailey", meaning bailiff, or from the Old English place-name Bailey, which translates as "berry wood".

Beryl (F)

Of Greek origin, and meaning "light green semiprecious gemstone".

Bich (F)

Of Vietnamese origin, meaning "gemstone".

Blossom (F)

The name Blossom is of Old English origin, and its meaning is "flower-like" and was first used in the 19th century as an affectionate pet name for a young girl.

Bluebell (F)

This woodland plant of the lily family produces clusters of bell-shaped blue flowers in Spring and is a popular choice as a name for girls born in the Spring.

Bradley (M)

Of Old English origin, meaning "broad meadow".

Brandon (M)

Of Old English origin, meaning "broom [shrub], gorse hill". Variant of the less popular Brendon.

Brooke (F)
Of Old English and Old German origin, meaning "water, small stream".

Bryony (F)
It is of Greek origin, and its meaning is "climbing plant".

Calla (F)
Of Greek origin, and meaning "beautiful", also the name of an elegant flower - the calla lily.

Chloe (F)
A Greek name meaning "green shoot". In Greek mythology Chloe is an epithet for the harvest goddess Demeter, and so the name Chloe is associated with plants.

Clover (F)
More commonly meaning "meadow flower, or wild flower", the name Clover is thought to have been derived from the Latin clava, meaning clubs. The mighty Hercules had a three-headed club, which the Clover leaf is supposed to resemble. The so-called clubs on playing cards are believed to have originated from the Clover leaf.

Crisanta (F)
Of Spanish and Greek origin, and its meaning is "golden flower."

Crystal (F)
This name is of Greek origin, and its meaning is "ice". Crystal is a transparent quartz gemstone, usually colourless, that can be cut to reflect brilliant light.

Dahlia (F)
Of Scandinavian origin, and its meaning is "valley". The Dahlia was the flower named for 18th-century Swedish botanist Anders Dahl.

Daisy (F)
Of Old English origin, and meaning "day's eye". It can be used as a nickname for Margaret, where in France, the flower is called a "marguerite".

Danica (F)
It is of Slavic origin, and means "morning star". There is a famous Royal Copenhagen china pattern known as "Flora Danica", or "Flowers of Denmark".

Darragh (M)
This name means "oak" and is derived from Gaelic.

Diamond (F)
Of English origin, it means "of high value, brilliant". The gemstone was first used as a given name in the 1890s. The gem is the birthstone for April, which makes it suitable for girls born in this month.

Dianthe (F)
Of Greek origin meaning "flower of the gods."

Douglas (M)
A name of Gaelic origin (from a Scottish clan name), meaning "dark stream".

Ebrel (F)

A Cornish name meaning the month of April.

Elodie (F)

Of French origin, it means "marsh flower".

Emerald (F)

Of English origin, it means "precious gemstone".

Esmeralda (F)

Of Spanish origin, meaning "emerald". It is a variant of Emerald, the prized green gemstone.

Evie (F)

The girl's name is a variant of Evelyn, meaning "life, animal".

Fleur (F)

Of French origin, it means "flower".

Flora (F)

Of Latin origin, meaning "flower". In mythology, Flora is the name of the Roman goddess of springtime.

Ford (M)

Adopted from the English surname, meaning "ford", as in a point where a river can be crossed on foot.

Forsythia (F)

A floral name for a brilliant yellow shrub that is one of the first signs of spring. Named for William Forsythe, the 18th-century botanist who classified it.

Gardenia (F)

Of English origin, a sweet-smelling flower named for the 18th-century Scottish naturalist Alexander Garden, who first classified it.

Garnet (F)
Of Middle English origin, a garnet is a dark red gemstone named for the pomegranate that the garnet crystals resemble.

George (M)
This name means "farmer, to work the earth", and is Greek in origin. It has been a popular name with British royalty since the eighteenth century and George III, was known as "Farmer George" for his interest in agriculture.

Giada (F)
An Italian name meaning "jade".

Guy (M)
Of Old German origin, meaning "wood",

Hari
This is one of the names of the Hindu god Vishnu. There are several meanings attached to this name including "brown, tawny, monkey, lion".

Heather (F)
Of Middle English origin, the name of an evergreen flowering plant that thrives on peaty barren lands.

Holly (F)
An English name from the evergreen holly shrub or tree. Holly sprigs are traditionally used as Christmas decorations and so this name is particularly associated with girls born around Christmas.

Hyacinth (F)
The name of a flower and a colour that ranges from sapphire to violet. See also Jacinta.

Ianthe (F)
In mythology, Ianthe was a sea nymph, the daughter of Oceanus, and the name means "violet flower".

Ignatius (M)

This Latin name, derived from the old Roman family name of Egnatius, means "fire".

Ilana (F)

A Hebrew name meaning "tree".

Ilima (F)

Of Hawaiian origin, meaning "the flower of Oahu."

Ione (F)

Of Greek origin, the name means "violet flower". variants include Iolanthe, and Yolanda is the more common Spanish form.

Iris (F)

Means "rainbow" in Greek. In Greek mythology Iris was a goddess associated with the rainbow who acted as a messenger for the gods. Also a plant genus covering several hundred species.

Isla (F)

A Scottish name meaning "from Islay" – the name of a Hebridean island.

Jacinta (F)

The Spanish form of Hyacinth, a name derived from the Greek mythological figure of Hyakinthos, from whose blood the flower was said to spring.

Jett (M)
Denoting a deep black colour from the English word "jet".

Jetta (F)
This name of Danish origin is a modern name and refers to jet, an intensely black, shiny gemstone.

Jolan (F)
Jolan is a variety of narcissus, closely related to the daffodil, and popular for girls born in the Spring. It first appeared in the 1940s.

Kaden (M)
A name of multiple meanings. Firstly, "companion" from Arabic, secondly it can be linked to a German surname meaning "fen" as in marshy land. It also has the meaning of "fighter" derived from an Irish Gaelic surname.

Kaimana (M)
This is a Hawaiian name meaning "power of the ocean". It can also be taken to mean "diamond" as it is the Hawaiian transcription of that word.

Kalei (F)
Of Hawaiian origin, meaning "a wreath of flowers".

Kalina (F)
Of Slavic origin, meaning "flower". The Hawaiian equivalent of Karen.

Kalinda
An Indian name meaning "the sun".

Krysanthe (F)
A popular name from Greece meaning "golden flower."

Lantana (F)
The name of an aromatic flower with tiny clusters of orange or purple blossoms.

Lauren (F)
An English name derived from the Latin word for "laurel".

Leilani (F)
It is of Hawaiian origin, and means "heavenly lei or royal child of heaven".

Lily (F)
Of Latin origin, the lily is a symbol of innocence and purity as well as beauty. Variations include Lillian.

Logan (M)
Adopted from the Scottish surname, this name means "little hollow" and takes it source from a Scottish place-name.

Malina (F)
A Polish, Czech and Slovak name meaning "raspberry".

Mansi (F)
Of Hopi origin, meaning "plucked flower."

Marigold (F)
Its source is an English expression meaning "A plant with bright orange and yellow flowers."

May (F)
Literally a month name; "May". May is also an English word for the hawthorn flower which blossoms in May.

Melantha (F)
A popular Greek name meaning "dark flower"

Nasrin (F)
A Persian name meaning "wild rose".

Nerola (F)
Of Italian origin, meaning "orange flower."

Nevada
Adopted from the American state of Nevada, which is Spanish for "snow-capped".

Oceana

A name of Greek origin meaning "ocean".

Oliver (M)

Of Latin origin, meaning "olive tree", the title character in the book by Charles Dickens.

Olivia (F)

Derived from the Latin word for "olive".

Opal (F)

Of Hindi and Sanskrit origin, it means "gem or jewel". A uniquely colourful iridescent gemstone, particularly suitable for an October baby as it is the birthstone for that month,

Pearl (F)

Of Latin origin, a pearl is a lustrous sphere formed within the shell of a pearl oyster, highly prized as a gem.

Petunia (F)

Flower name for a humble-looking flower with white or pink blossoms.

Philantha (F)

A popular Greek name meaning "lover of flowers."

Poppy (F)

Of Latin origin, one of the more popular names for girls in recent years, taken from the flower.

Primrose (F)

Of Middle English origin meaning "first rose", a flower which blooms early in spring.

Qamar (M)

An Arabic name meaning "moon".

Rosa (F)

Popular flower name for girls that has many variants.

Rose (F)

A very popular floral name, variants of which include Rosa.

Roselaine (F)

Of English and Latin origin, meaning "rose".

Roxanne (F)

It is of Persian origin, and means "dawn".

Ruby (F)

Of English origin, meaning "the red gemstone" this name, popular in England in the 1950s is now extremely popular.

Saffron (F)

Part of the crocus family, and also used as a spice as well as a bright orange-yellow colour dye. Popularized in the 1960s in the song by Donovan "Mellow Yellow".

Sapphire (F)

Adopted from the blue birthstone of September.

Savannah (F)

This is a name of Spanish origin which arose from a native South American word for a "treeless plain". The name can also be taken to honour the cities of Savannah in Georgia and South Carolina.

Sequoia (F)
Of Cherokee origin, meaning "sparrow". Also the name of the giant redwood tree, named for a Cherokee Indian of the early 19th century.

Sienna (F)
After the distinctive hue of the clay found in the Italian city of Siena, which isbrownish-yellow when raw, and reddish-brown when burnt.

Sharon (F)
It is of Hebrew origin, and meanings "a fertile plain". In the bible, The Song of Solomon describes the Schulamite woman as a flower of Sharon.

Silas (M)
A short form of Silvanus, a Latin name meaning "wood, forest". In Roman mythology Silvanus was the god of forests.

Skye (F)
A Scottish place-name – the Isle of Skye off Scotland's west coast. Also a form of the English name "Sky", meaning literally "sky".

Stella (F)
From Latin, meaning "star".

Sterling
This name comes from Old English and means "little star".

Tabitha (F)
Meaning "gazelle", this biblical name is of Aramaic origin.

Tallulah (F)
This is a Native American name meaning "leaping water".

Tamar (F)
A Hebrew name meaning "palm tree".

Tane (M)
A Maori name meaning "man". In Polynesian mythology Tane is the god of forests, and according to legend he created the first man.

Tasi

Meaning "sea, ocean" in the Chamorro language of Guam, Micronesia.

Tor (M)

A Scandinavian name meaning "thunder". This name comes from Thor, the Old Norse god of thunder and war.

Twyla (F)

It is of English origin and is a variant of Twila, meaning "twilight, early evening".

Ume (F)

A Japanese name meaning "plum blossom", a symbol of devotion in Japanese culture.

Vance (M)

This is from a surname meaning "marshland" and is of Old English origin.

Violet (F)

Of Latin origin, the descriptive name not only of a flower, but also a colour. Popular since the 1830s.

Willow (F)

An English name from the willow tree, in all likelihood adopted as a given name because of the willow tree's graceful appearance.

Xeni (F)

Of guatemalan origin, meaning "protector of plants and flowers".

Xuan (M)

A Vietnamese name meaning "spring".

Xylia (F)

This name means "of the forest" or "woods-dweller" and is derived from Greek.

Yazmin (F)

A Persian name for "jasmine", the fragrant climbing plant.

Yolanda (F)

Of Spanish origin, this name means "violet flower".

Yves (M)

Meaning "yew", this is a French name of Germanic origin.

Zahara (F)

This Arabic name means "flowering".

Zahra (F)

This variant of Zahara is also Arabic and means "white flower".

Zinnia (F)

Of Latin origin, the Zinnia was named for 18th-century German botanist Johann Zinn who classified it.

Zuzanna (F)

A Polish and Latvian form of Susanna, which comes from the Hebrew name Shoshana meaning "lily".

Adam

A Hebrew name meaning "man". According to the Bible, Adam was the first human, created by God from the earth.

Aidan

It is of Gaelic origin, meaning "fire".

Alexander

Meaning "man's defender and helper" this name is Greek in origin. A famous bearer of this name was Alexander the Great, who in the fourth century BC conquered most of the known world.

Alfie

This is a pet form of the Old English name Alfred, and has latterly become a given name in its own right. Alfred means "elf counsel".

Benjamin

From the Old Testament, Benjamin is a Hebrew name meaning "son of the right hand" or "son of the south", or "son of my old age".

Brandon

Of Old English origin, meaning "broom [shrub], gorse hill". Variant of the less popular Brendon.

Callum

This is a Gaelic form of the Latin name Columba, meaning "dove", the symbol of peace and gentleness. Saint Columba was a sixth-century Irish missionary who was behind Scotland's conversion to Christianity.

Cameron

A Gaelic name meaning "crooked nose", adopted from the surname of the Scottish Cameron clan.

Charles

Of Old German origin, meaning "free man". Charles and its variant forms have been favoured by the royalty of several countries for several centuries, including the present Prince of Wales.

Conner

Of Gaelic origin, meaning "hound-lover". The name of a legendary king of Ulster who lived at the time of Christ.

Daniel

Of Hebrew origin, meaning "God is my judge". In the old Testament, Daniel was a Hebrew prophet living in Babylon where he served in the court of the king, interpreting his dreams. He was persecuted for his faith in God, which kept him alive in a den of lions.

Declan

Of Irish origin, the name of an Irish 6th century saint.

Dexter

An adopted occupational surname which means "dyer" in Old English, although Dexter is probably known better for its co-incidental Latin meaning of "skillful, right-handed".

Dylan
Of Welsh origin, meaning "son of the sea". In Welsh mythology Dylan is the son of the virgin goddess Aranrhod. It is also the name of one of Wales most famous sons, Dylan Thomas.

Ethan
The name of a wise man in the Old Testament, this Hebrew name means "firm, enduring".

Finlay
From the Gaelic name Fionnlagh, meaning "fair warrior".

Fred
A variant of Alfred (Old English) and Frederick (Old German), and the meaning of Fred is "elf or magical counsel".

George
This name means "farmer, to work the earth", and is Greek in origin. It has been a popular name with British royalty since the eighteenth century and George III, was known as "Farmer George" for his interest in agriculture.

Guy
Of Old German origin, meaning "wood".

Harrison
Of Old English origin, meaning "son of Harry".

Harry
Used as a nickname of Henry and Harold, of Old German origin meaning "home ruler". Fictional character Harry Potter has also influenced the name and Prince Henry of Wales is widely known as Harry.

Harvey
Of Old English and Old French origin, meaning "eager for battle; strong and worthy".

Isaac
A Hebrew name meaning "he laughs".

Jack

This has evolved from a medieval English pet name for John. So the meaning of Jack is linked to that of the Hebrew name John, which is "God is gracious".

Jake

This English name developed in the Middle Ages as a version of Jack, but is now used as a given name in its own right. Also, Jake can be used as a pet form of Jacob.

James

Of English origin, James is a variant of Jacob and as such means the same, i.e "he who supplants". The King James Bible is named in reference to James I of England (16th-17th century) who commissioned the translation into English of what has become the primary faith document of many Christians today.

Joseph

This name is an English form of the Hebrew name Yosef, and means "God will increase". The name Joseph is borne by several major biblical figures including Joseph of Arimathea who took Jesus down from the cross and buried him.

Kyle

Of Gaelic origin, meaning "narrow, straight".

Liam

This is an Irish short form of William, a name of Germanic origin which can be interpreted as meaning "strong protector".

Luke

This biblical name is of Greek origin and means "man from Lucania" (a region in Italy). In the New Testament, Luke is a disciple of Jesus and a doctor. Luke is the patron saint of physicians and surgeons.

Mark

Of Latin origin, meaning "dedicated to Mars", Mark was the writer of one of the gospels.

Matthew

Meaning "gift of God", this name is of Hebrew origin.

Max

Meaning "greatest", this Latin name is derived from an ancient Roman family name.

Michael

Of Hebrew origin, meaning "who resembles God". In the Bible, Michael is an archangel who leads the army of heaven, and Saint Michael is the patron saint of soldiers.

Miles

From the Old German "merciful; eager to please".

Oliver

Of Latin origin, meaning "olive tree", the title character in the book by Charles Dickens.

Oscar

This name may be of Scandinavian origin and be associated with divinity, meaning "god spear".

It could also be derived from Gaelic and mean "deer-lover". In Irish legend, Oscar was the grandson of the hero Fionn mac Cumhail.

Ryan

It is of Gaelic origin, meaning "king".

Samuel

Meaning "God has heard" this name is of Hebrew origin. The biblical Samuel was a major Hebrew judge and prophet who established the Hebrew monarchy.

Sebastian

This name means "man from Sebaste" being derived from a Roman Christian martyr who came from Sebaste, a town in Asia Minor. "Sebaste" comes from the Greek word for "venerable".

Silas

A short form of Silvanus, a Latin name meaning "wood, forest". In Roman mythology Silvanus was the god of forests.

Thomas

This name is derived from Greek and Aramaic and means "twin". In the New Testament Thomas is a disciple of Jesus who is initially reluctant to accept Christ's resurrection.

Toby

Of English origin, short form of Tobias, meaning "the Lord is good".

Zachary

This name means "God remembers", and is derived from the Hebrew name Zechariah, a name borne by an Old Testament prophet.

Abigail
A biblical, Hebrew name meaning "joyful".

Alyssa
From the herbaceous plant alyssum, which are beautiful, delicate plants that come in a variety of colours, most typically yellow or white.

Amelia
Of Latin and Old German origin, meaning "industrious; striving".

Amy
Of Latin origin, Amy means "beloved" and is an English version of the Old French name Amée.

Caitlin
A Gaelic form of Katharine, meaning "pure".

Chloe
A Greek name meaning "green shoot". In Greek mythology Chloe is an epithet for the harvest goddess Demeter, and so the name Chloe is associated with plants.

Daisy
Of Old English origin, and meaning "day's eye". It can be used as a nickname for Margaret, where in France, the flower is called a "marguerite".

Danielle

Of Hebrew and French origin, and its meaning is "God is my Judge". Feminine variant of Daniel.

Ella

Meaning "bright light" is a popular name in all English speaking countries, regularly making the 'top names' lists and is also popular in Norwegian and Swedish speaking countries.

Ellie

Ellie means "sun ray; bright light" and is of Old German and Greek origin.

Emily

This is the femine of Emilio and as such means the same, i.e "rival". It is derived from the Roman family name "Aemilius".

Emma

It is of Old French and Old German origin, and its meaning is "entire or universal".

Erin

Meaning "Ireland", derived from "Eire", the Gaelic word for Ireland.

Evie

The girl's name is a variant of Evelyn, meaning "life, animal".

Freya

In Norse mythology Freya is the goddess of love and beauty. Her name means "lady".

Georgia

Of Greek origin, this is the feminine form of George.

Grace

An English "virtue name" meaning "grace", in the sense of "the grace of God". To modern ears "Grace" is also suggestive of gracious manners and elegance.

Hannah

A Hebrew name meaning "God has favoured me". In the Old Testament Hannah is the mother of the prophet Samuel.

Imogen

Meaning "maiden", Imogen is the name of a princess in Shakespeare's play **Cymbeline**. It is a name of Gaelic origin and is derived from the figure of Innogen, from Celtic legend.

Isabella

Of Spanish and Latin origin, a variant of Elizabeth from the Hebrew meaning "God's promise, God is my oath".

Jessica

Of uncertain meaning, Jessica is probably derived from the Hebrew Old Testament name Jesca. The name Jessica appears to have been invented by Shakespeare (for Shylock's daughter in **The Merchant of Venice**).

Katherine

From the word "katharos" meaning "pure" in Greek.

Lauren

An English name derived from the Latin word for "laurel".

Layla

An Arabic name meaning "night". Made popular by the song of the same name by Eric Clapton.

Leah (F)

It is of Hebrew origin, and its meaning is "delicate". Biblically, Leah was the name of Jacob's first wife.

Leilani

It is of Hawaiian origin, and means "heavenly lei or royal child of heaven".

Lily

Of Latin origin, the lily is a symbol of innocence and purity as well as beauty. Variations include Lillian.

Lola

A Spanish pet form of Dolores, meaning "sorrows". Dolores comes from the Spanish title for the Virgin Mary – **María de los Dolores** ("Mary of Sorrows").

Lucy
Derived from Latin and meaning "light".

Maisie
A nickname for Margaret of Old English origin, meaning "pearl".

Mia
An Italian name meaning "mine".

Molly
Of Irish origin, a nickname of Mary (Latin) "star of the sea". In use since the late Middle Ages. In the past has had negative connotations given that "moll" means a prostitute or a gangster's girlfriend.

Olivia
Derived from the Latin word for "olive".

Phoebe
This name means "bright", and is of Greek origin.

Poppy
Of Latin origin, one of the more popular names for girls in recent years, taken from the flower.

Rebekah
The name Rebekah is a variant of Rebecca, the meaning of which is "to bind". In the book of Genesis the account of Rebekah is of a maiden of beauty, modesty, and kindness who became the wife of Abraham's son, Isaac.

Rhianna
A Welsh name meaning "great queen" or "goddess". Rhianna is a form of Rhiannon, who is the goddess of fertility and the moon in Welsh mythology.

Rose
A very popular floral name, variants of which include Rosa.

Ruby
Of English origin, meaning "the red gemstone" this name, popular in England in the 1950s is now extremely popular.

Serena
A Latin name meaning "serene, calm".

Stella
From Latin, meaning "star".

Victoria
From Latin origins, this name means "victory".

Zara
Of Arabic origin, meaning "radiance".

INDEX

A-Z Names

A-Z Names

A-Z Names

Boys Names

Girls Names

Girls Names   Biblical

Cultural Origins

Ace (M) - pp 19
Aidan (M) - pp 19
Alexander (M) - pp 19
Alexis (F) - pp 19
Alfie (M) - pp 19
Alice (F) - pp 19
Alison (F) - pp 19
Amber (F) - pp 19
Amelia (F) - pp 20
Amy (F) - pp 20
Angharad (F) - pp 20
Anne (F) - pp 20
Antonio (M) - pp 20
Antony (M) - pp 20
Anya (F) - pp 20
Asa (M) - pp 20
Ashanti (F) - pp 21
Ava (F) - pp 21
Beatrix (F) - pp 21
Beau (M) - pp 21
Bethany (F) - pp 21
Blair (M) - pp 21
Blythe (F) - pp 21
Bradley (M) - pp 21
Bran (M) - pp 21
Brandon (M) - pp 22
Brianna (F) - pp 22
Brice - pp 22
Caitlin (F) - pp 22
Callum (M) - pp 22
Cameron (M) - pp 22
Candida (F) - pp 22
Carl (M) - pp 22
Carys (F) - pp 22
Cato (M) - pp 22
Charles (M) - pp 23
Charlotte (F) - pp 23

Conner (M) - pp 23
Courtney (F) - pp 23
Dakota (F) - pp 23
Dale (M) - pp 23
Daniel (M) - pp 23
Danielle (F) - pp 24
Darcy (F) - pp 24
Darragh (M) - pp 24
David (M) - pp 24
Deborah (F) - pp 24
Declan (M) - pp 24
Delaney (M) - pp 24
Delilah (F) - pp 24
Dexter (M) - pp 24
Dominic (M) - pp 25
Douglas (M) - pp 25
Dylan (M) - pp 25
Earl (M) - pp 25
Ebele (F) - pp 25
Ebrel (F) - pp 25
Edward (M) - pp 25
Elijah (M) - pp 25
Elizabeth (F) - pp 25
Ella (F) - pp 25
Ellie (F) - pp 26
Ellis (M) - pp 26
Emer (F) - pp 26
Emilio (M) - pp 26
Emily (F) - pp 26
Emma (F) - pp 26
Eric (M) - pp 26
Erin (F) - pp 26
Euan (M) - pp 27
Evander (M) - pp 27
Evie (F) - pp 27
Faith (F) - pp 27
Fallon (F) - pp 27

Felicity (F) - pp 27
Felix (M) - pp 27
Fiona (F) - pp 27
Finlay (M) - pp 27
Ford (M) - pp 27
Fred (M) - pp 27
Frederick (M) - pp 28
Gabriella (F) - pp 28
Galen (M) - pp 28
Geneviève (F) - pp 28
George (M) - pp 28
Georgia (F) - pp 28
Gerard (M) - pp 28
Geronimo (M) - pp 28
Giada (F) - pp 28
Giselle (F) - pp 29
Gita (F) - pp 29
Grace (F) - pp 29
Hari - pp 29
Harrison (M) - pp 29
Harry (M) - pp 29
Harvey (M) - pp 29
Heidi (F) - pp 29
Henrietta (F) - pp 29
Holly (F) - pp 30
Hope (F) - pp 30
Hugo (M) - pp 30
Ignatius (M) - pp 30
Imogen (F) - pp 30
Isaac (M) - pp 30
Isadora (F) - pp 30
Isabella (F) - pp 31
Isaiah (M) - pp 31
Isla (F) - pp 31
Jack (M) - pp 31
Jacob (M) - pp 31
Jake (M) - pp 31

Cultural Origins

James (M) - pp 31
Jay (M) - pp 31
Jennifer (F) - pp 32
Jeremiah (M) - pp 32
Jett (M) - pp 32
Jody (F) - pp 32
Joel (M) - pp 32
Joseph (M) - pp 32
Julian (M) - pp 32
Juliet (F) - pp 32
Kaden (M) - pp 32
Kaimana (M) - pp 33
Kalinda - pp 33
Kallista (F) - pp 33
Kalyan (M) - pp 33
Katherine (F) - pp 33
Keely (F) - pp 33
Keira - pp 33
Kent (M) - pp 33
Kerenza (F) - pp 33
Kevin (M) - pp 33
Khalid (M) - pp 34
Kieran (M) - pp 34
Kizziah - pp 34
Kim (F) - pp 34
Kofi (M) - pp 34
Kurt (M) - pp 34
Kyle (M) - pp 34
Laetitia (F) - pp 34
Lalita (F) - pp 34
Lauren (F) - pp 34
Layla (F) - pp 34
Leilani (F) - pp 35
Leo (M) - pp 35
Leona (F) - pp 35
Levi (M) - pp 35
Lewis (M) - pp 35

Liam (M) - pp 35
Lisa (F) - pp 35
Liv (F) - pp 35
Llewellyn (M) - pp 35
Lola (F) - pp 35
Logan (M) - pp 35
Louis (M) - pp 36
Lucy (F) - pp 36
Luke (M) - pp 36
Mabel (F) - pp 36
Madeleine (F) - pp 36
Madison (F) - pp 36
Maisie (F) - pp 36
Malika (F) - pp 36
Malina (F) - pp 37
Malory (F) - pp 37
Marcus (M) - pp 37
Mark (M) - pp 37
Matilda (F) - pp 37
Maverick (M) - pp 37
Max (M) - pp 37
May (F) - pp 37
Megan (F) - pp 37
Melanie (F) - pp 37
Mercedes (F) - pp 38
Meredith (F) - pp 38
Mia (F) - pp 38
Michael (M) - pp 38
Miguel (M) - pp 38
Miles (M) - pp 38
Milo (M) - pp 38
Miranda (F) - pp 38
Mohammed (M) - pp 38
Molly (F) - pp 38
Montgomery (M) - pp 39
Morven - pp 39
Nasrin (F) - pp 39

Natalie (F) - pp 39
Natasha (F) - pp 39
Niall (M) - pp 39
Niamh (F) - pp 39
Nicholas (M) - pp 39
Noah (M) - pp 39
Nye (M) - pp 40
Oceana - pp 40
Oliver (M) - pp 40
Olivia (F) - pp 40
Omorose (F) - pp 40
Orlando (M) - pp 40
Oscar (M) - pp 40
Owain (M) - pp 40
Owen (M) - pp 40
Paige (F) - pp 40
Patricia (F) - pp 41
Penelope (F) - pp 41
Peregrine (M) - pp 41
Phoebe (F) - pp 41
Piers (M) - pp 41
Pip (M) - pp 41
Portia (F) - pp 42
Primo (M) - pp 42
Qamar (M) - pp 42
Quincy - pp 42
Quinn (M) - pp 42
Quy - pp 42
Rachel (F) - pp 42
Randolph (M) - pp 42
Rebekah (F) - pp 42
Reece (M) - pp 42
Regan (F) - pp 43
Rex (M) - pp 43
Rhianna (F) - pp 43
Rhys (M) - pp 43
Richard (M) - pp 43

Cultural Origins

Literature/Arts

Myths & Legends   Nature

Nature